Killer Snakes

Python

By Daisy Allyn

Gareth Stevens
Publishing

Please visit our Web site, www.garethstevens.com. For a free color catalog of all our high-quality books, call toll free 1-800-542-2595 or fax 1-877-542-2596.

Library of Congress Cataloging-in-Publication Data

Allyn, Daisy.
Python / Daisy Allyn.
    p. cm. — (Killer snakes)
Includes index.
ISBN 978-1-4339-4560-1 (pbk.)
ISBN 978-1-4339-4561-8 (6-pack)
ISBN 978-1-4339-4559-5 (library binding)
1. Pythons—Juvenile literature. I. Title.
QL666.O67A45 2011
597.96'78—dc22

                                    2010030693

First Edition

Published in 2011 by
Gareth Stevens Publishing
111 East 14th Street, Suite 349
New York, NY 10003

Designer: Michael J. Flynn
Editor: Greg Roza

Photo credits: Cover, pp. 1, (2–4, 6–8, 10, 12, 14, 16, 18, 20–24 snake skin texture), 4–5, 6–7, 13, 17, 19, 21 Shutterstock.com; p. 9 iStockphoto.com; p. 11 Oxford Scientific/Photolibrary/Getty Images; p. 15 Werner Bollmann/Photolibrary/Getty Images.

Printed in the United States of America

CPSIA compliance information: Batch #CW11GS: For further information contact Gareth Stevens, New York, New York at 1-800-542-2595.

Contents

Boldface words appear in the glossary.

Big Snakes!

Pythons are large, strong snakes. There are 28 kinds of pythons in the world. They live in hot areas in Asia, Africa, and Australia. Pythons are good swimmers. They can also climb trees. Pythons kill by **squeezing** their **prey**!

The Longest Snake

The reticulated (rih-TIH-kyuh-lay-tuhd) python is the longest snake in the world. It can be more than 30 feet (9.1 m) long and weigh 350 pounds (159 kg)! The reticulated python gets its name from the **patterns** on its skin. Something that is reticulated has criss-crossed lines.

Python Babies

Female reticulated pythons lay eggs. A large reticulated python may lay up to 100 eggs at one time. After the female lays the eggs, she **coils** around them to keep them warm. Baby snakes break out of the eggs in about 85 days.

Once the baby reticulated pythons break out of their eggs, the mother leaves them. Each snake is about 30 inches (76 cm) long. Their colors help them hide from enemies such as hawks and cobras. Baby reticulated pythons eat mice, rats, lizards, and frogs.

Made for Hunting

Pythons are good hunters. They can see and smell very well. They use their tongues to smell. Pythons also have special parts on their faces called pits. Pits help pythons feel the heat of passing prey.

13

The prey a python hunts depends on the python's size. Smaller pythons eat small animals, such as frogs and lizards. Reticulated pythons eat birds and rats. However, sometimes they eat larger animals, such as pigs and deer!

Python Teeth

Just like most snakes, pythons have two sharp teeth called fangs. However, pythons don't use their teeth to kill. Python teeth are hooked. The shape of a python's teeth helps the snake hold on to its prey.

Sneaky Snake

A python often hides and waits for prey to go by. The python bites the prey and holds on. It quickly wraps its long body around the animal. Then it squeezes so hard the animal can't breathe. After the animal has died, the python swallows it in one gulp!

Pythons and People

Pythons don't often **attack** people. In some places, pythons are used to kill pests, such as rats. Some people like to keep pythons as pets! Other people like to wear belts, boots, and coats made of python skin.

Snake Facts
Reticulated Python

Length	some can be more than 30 feet (9.1 m) long
Weight	up to 350 pounds (159 kg)
Where It Lives	Africa, Asia, Australia; hot places
Life Span	25 to 30 years
Killer Fact	The longest snake ever recorded was a reticulated python found in Indonesia in 1902. It was nearly 33 feet (10 m) long!

Glossary

attack: to try to harm someone or something

coil: to wrap around something many times

pattern: the way colors or shapes happen over and over again

prey: an animal hunted by other animals for food

squeeze: to press something tightly

For More Information

Books

Goldish, Meish. *Reticulated Python: The World's Longest Snake.* New York, NY: Bearport Publishing, 2010.

Gunderson, Megan M. *Pythons.* Edina, MN: ABDO Publishing, 2011.

Web Sites

Reptiles: Python

www.sandiegozoo.org/animalbytes/t-python.html
Read about pythons and find out how they are different from other snakes.

Reticulated Pythons

animal.discovery.com/fansites/crochunter/ australiazoo/40reticpython.html
Learn more about the reticulated python.

Index